Shadow Songs

Erica Adelaide Johnson

ISBN: 978-1-7355967-0-9

Photographs and cover design by Erica Adelaide Johnson.

For those that dared to see a light in me even on my darkest days. You helped me find healing from the pain that inspired these words.

Table of Contents

Introduction

I've sat hushed in the dark watching the shadows of strangers dancing on the walls as the cold crept in. I've heard the quiet breaking of my own heart and the straining of a bending soul under the weight of it all. The ice formed thick on my heart after countless cold shoulders were turned on me. I wondered and worried if somehow I was incapable of offering my sincere forgiveness. I sought to bring an end to the storm I had been weathering for the better part of five years. I knew that finding such forgiveness within myself was the only way that the turmoil could ever really give way to peace.

You should know there is fire in you, not merely to drive you forward, but also to thaw those parts of yourself that you thought might be lost to you. This is for all those souls out there shying away from the light as they watch the midnight footsteps beyond their door. I hope someday you realize that your shadow songs are worthy. The painful symphony created in your darkness can give way to the artful beauty of a new beginning. The imprints and silhouettes on the walls are yours to control. You are more than your circumstance. You do not have to sit in your tragedy alone. You can brave the light.

Here you will find a journey, in the form of poetry, from the dark, damp depths to the warm firelight. We all must face our seasons. Some will feel hopeless, others will convince you that you're invincible. Your dark times are nothing to feel shame for. They are only a stepping stone on your path to find the light that has lived inside you your entire life.

I think someone somewhere needed this. I know I did. So, this is for you. I hope it helps.

Part 1: Darkness

Section 1: The Breaking

It always fades.

I watched as the firelight faded to glowing coals
Willing the wind to breathe life back into the flame
For just a moment more.

The air sat heavy on my skin.
The fading is inevitable
Joy, pain, adrenaline,
Loneliness, laughter, even love,
At least the easy kind.

Memories. Those fade too,
And that will prove to be the worst of it.
Cling to a feeling, fight to preserve
A version of ourselves lost to time.

Sands to cement.

Seems like a lifetime ago
Since this house was still.
Chaos erupted, swept through this space.
The magnitude of one instant of change
Turned the sands of this hourglass to cement.

Reality once taken for granted
Now lost in the past.
I find myself hiding in the rubble
From the blame you so carelessly cast on me.

Once honey-coated lullabies.

I never saw it coming.
The words dripped like poison from your lips.
Once honey-coated lullabies
Now daggers aimed to
Bleed me dry.

Heartache and frustration
Tinge my every thought.
A pain you can never know
Born from love stripped away
Left bare to feel its weight.

I used to feel compassion
For the life you wanted that never came.
But it is your choice
Alone to throw it away,
To throw us all away.

No more backward glances
Casting rope to you
Nearly drowning as you try to pull me in too.
This is my turn to fly free.

Cut myself loose.
Let go of me.

Slow drowning.

It is the slow drowning,
The doomed treading of water
Towards an ever distant shore,
The fight with the horizon
As it swallows the sun once more.

Limbs laid heavy.

Limbs laid heavy
Blanketed in snow
Suspended by the
Think haze of winter day.
I still cannot
See you but I feel
The weight of you
In this place.
My limbs laid heavy too
With the invisible presence of you.

Absence.

How strange it is
That the presence
Of another need not
Be consciously noticed
For their absence
To be felt.

Known by another.

How haunting it is to watch
A life once so prevalent in your own
Glide by without a glance,
No notion of what once existed
The palpable knowledge of being known by another
The very essence of tragedy
Found in the transition of seasons.

Almost.

Almost. You were almost there for me,
But you turned the corner
Got lost in the crowd.
You had other obligations.
I guess I understand.
But sometimes, on the bad days,
I still miss the feel of your hand.

Remnants.

I cannot bear it
To sit idly by
Watch in silence
As you snuff out
The remnants of love
In this place.
So, I turn my gaze
From the stranger
As they speak my name.

Crumbling.

There is no tenderness to be mustered
The rock I have been for so long
Begins to crack.
Can't you see?
I am crumbling,
Becoming the very rubble that once smothered me.

Cold shoulder.

I cannot seem to turn away
From the anger in your eyes.
I am a moth to the flame
Caught in your trap for all time.
I will flutter aimlessly
Bash myself against your cold shoulder
A thousand times more.
Bruised and weary I will fly
Towards the light,
But it is always you.
It's just you.
You and your entrancing glow.

Invisible.

I have tried so desperately
To become the kind of invisible
That I always felt was my place.
Somehow, they still see me,
Vulnerable in this cage.
I find myself cornered by good intentions,
Forever struggling to escape.

Let me tend my garden in peace.

I can't seem to harden my heart to you.
You work to dismantle the walls I have built
The ones I labored over,
Carved from stone myself.
Inside I planted the last seed I could salvage
The final remnant of the heart of me.
Why can't you, won't you leave me be?
Let me tend my garden in peace.

Reflections.

Reflections of sunsets captured in cheap sunglasses,
Life a mere collection of crystal memories.
Shattered reality perfectly preserved
Yet untouchable, trapped in the past.
How long have I stared into this glass?

A tantalizingly painful notion
That you might exist in your prior form
Lost somewhere on the other side of a mirror
Perhaps in the depths of an old photograph.
I am haunted by what I may never know as truth.

Who are you? Who were you?
It's all smoke and mirrors past,
But I cannot break this glass.
Refuse to shatter what could have, should have been
Into shards of brokenness.

Mist.

The mist clings to the mountainside
Like the heat to your skin
Like I to you
In this strong wind.

Not still.

No one could break me,
Not like you.
Bend me to my knees
Face pressed against the floorboards
Grit of dust on my teeth.
Pound my fists
One, two, three times more.
Pour it out
What I should not have to bear,
Not still.

Smooth out my edges.

Wasted. How much have I wasted?
Energy and time
Devoted to the meaningless pursuit,
The search for some reasoning
An explanation for your actions
All those years ago.
And now
The loud, glaring now
That I have never been able to escape.

The understanding is still
Lost on me.
I can find no cause
Not one that will
Ever satisfy my soul.

How can I smooth out my edges
When you're still here
Chipping away at me?
Filling my mind with uncertainty,
The idea that I
Am insignificant in this.

Impossibility in my madness.

You. I do not know how to write about you.
The person who I have given myself to
When the idea of trusting another soul seemed impossible.
That's you. The impossibility in my madness
The unlikely idea that love might survive
In the wake of disaster,
That despite the shadow I inevitably cast
You might still squint at my light,
The light I thought had long since flickered out,
Here you are.
And I am cruel, even with my best intentions.
You are an innocent caught in the crossfire
Of my wretched thoughts.
I cannot be good at loving you.
I can only promise to be
In the moments of clarity, unwavering.
I did choose you.
I still choose you.

Rock planted on my lap.

I don't want to just sit here
Rock planted on my lap
As the waters rush in.
But I chose this didn't I?
Or did I simply relinquish my choice?
Are they perhaps the same?

Numb.

The night seemed alive and wild somehow
Even in the thick of winter
Standing in the glow of the moon.
I felt the chill against my skin
Shivered as it radiated through.
For the first time
In so, so long
It make me feel alive too
Not merely numb.

Winter wind.

Whispers drift in
Soft on the winter wind
Touch my ear lightly
Like the laughter of a long lost friend.

Lost and found.

The longer I wander through the dark forest
The more I believe that lost and found
Are mere perceptions,
Our feeble attempt to assign some concrete placement
To an endlessly flowing journey.

This life is but a river.
We are simply caught in the current.
Sometimes the waters grow still,
A peaceful moment before the rapids.
Wherever the current leads, I will face it with you.

Occupied space.

All we can hope is that a whisper of light
Might break through
These shadows of doubt.

That we might find a reason
To believe in the improbable idea
That we are in fact more,

Than just an occupied space.

To the bones of me.

I've wondered often
Just how to find true rest.
In the absence of activity
I am still filled to the brim.
Overflowing, stationary chaos
Tired from the inability
To treasure an idle moment.
Makes me long for them even
More.
But that is what I should be running towards,
More. There is so much more,
To do. To feel. To be.
Before the time of more of them is here
So that there is less of me.
But don't misunderstand me
I crave more to the bones of me.
But I am frightened of more
So why is less so maddening?

I swam.

When tragedy strikes the seconds sludge past.
I could not close my eyes.
There was no turning from it.
Mere feet from me I watched
As everything collapsed.
I was engulfed in the debris
The ugly, burning air that singed me from the outside in.
I felt the tilt,
Then the sharp break.
Or maybe that was just innocence giving way.
The world came crashing in
Swept me away in the waves of bitterness.
The current so strong it turned my memory sour.
I could do nothing but fight my way to the surface,
The truest form of sink or swim.
Somewhere on the horizon was the blinking of a lifeboat
So I swam.

Section 2: Embracing the Dark

For your ghost.

I cannot accept what others have chosen to ignore,
Pretend that I am not
Forever at the mercy of your selfishness.

I've grown so tired
Of living this lie,
Twisted story like a serpent in my mind.

Choked my bones with an invisible tightening
I felt strangled in an empty room
Caught up in the slow slide toward oblivion.

After all this time,
Salt water still paints the ground for your ghost,
But never for your shadow.

Wildfires.

My cheeks act as a canvas
For the tear-tracked masterpiece crafted
Born of the salt water that washed away the soot
From the bridges I have burned.
There are wildfires blazing in these eyes of mine,
But this scorch is far from sinister.

It is the sustenance of the hearth
Constructed in my core, burning low and hot
Keeping me warm
Through the coldest winter I've ever known.

Sands of you.

I've watched everything I'd ever known
Turn to sand and slip through the cracks.
Now I am nothing but an empty hourglass.

You turned me upside down
Made me brand new
Filled me up with the sands of you.

Now my soul lies with the shore.
It is peace. It is power.
And the precious balance of both.

A jar or two to share.

My words are not always beautiful.
They do not flow like honey
A constant, smooth stream of gold.
They are at times fickle
Slow to pour forth on the page.
So I wait and I long for the taste
To gather a jar or two to share
That my gifts might find themselves used,
For I have a fear of idle hands and thoughts.

Stolen years cast shadows.

Silence used to trouble me
Too much space for this old creaking house,
For the house that used to be my home,
Was never actually my home.

Can I adopt the same reverence for all those years
I'd like to pretend were not mine? Now I can't rest,
Can't take a breath
Without the panic of one more wasted second.
Stolen years cast shadows, no matter where I go.

It's never far enough.
Never enough.
Will it ever be enough?
Will I?

I can't hear my own voice.
She's gaged in the corner over there,
Hiding in the shadows waiting to break these shackles,
I hope.

Cricket songs.

My days are filled with cricket songs
And the incessant ticking of clocks.

Shall I linger a few moments more
Stare longingly at the door
Carve marks into the table and wait?

Cast spiteful glances in the mirror
Make an enemy of my own mind
Drive myself to madness and wait?

Tracks worn into the carpet
Pacing to an unheard beat
Drums echo the call.

I long for you on days like this
To cease the noise with your silence.

Until one day it breaks through.

The fleeting present rushes by me.
I am caught up in the ever imminent
Glances of what once was,
Or perhaps what I only imagined it was.
The inevitable future looms over me
Beyond what I believe I can endure.
I wonder if the weight will always
Crush me in my place
Until one day it breaks through these ribs
To meet me full strength
No longer looming on the horizon,
Buries itself in me
Makes its presence known.
Is that eternity?

What lies between.

It is the darkness between the moments of light
That we must prepare ourselves for.
When the world grows quiet
How loud are your thoughts?
Mine are deafening.
I've been fighting the tug
Of misery at my sleeve
Even in moments of joy.
What lies between
The space of two breaths
Two blinks
The space between heartbeats?
Darling, at times, it is dark.
And it demands to be felt.

Match her depth.

He vowed he'd never sink again
But still couldn't quite match her depth
Until the silt was flush with his skin
The weight of her surrounding him.
She controlled the tide
Hung the only stars in his sky
Left him drowning in her darkness
Kissed his heart with light
Taught him to breathe deep
In the watery depths.
She the sea he was lost in.

For a lifetime, I'm sure.

How do I shoulder it
The affliction that keeps on giving
Does not blink or waver
With the passage of time?
See I can bear it
For a lifetime, I'm sure.
But an eternity?
That is much more,
To never know again
What I swear I knew.
That was you.

The difference.

I cannot pretend
That I do not still feel it
The loud absence of you
Strongest on the days
That should be the happiest.
But even when you speak
I never truly hear from you.

So, I find myself apologizing
To the few that do see me.
My happiness cannot be
What they think it should.
The difference is but another
Thing that was stolen from me.

Bittersweet.

Life has called to me
Bittersweet.
The realization of moments,
Memories slipping past.
In the midst of crowds
I have always felt it
Like sand in my grasp.
Meaning is made here
Precious in context.

I just never knew
So much of my past
Would lose too much of its sweetness,
That you might turn so bitter.

Days skim past.

The more I try to pull my pieces
Together from the ends of the earth
The more I feel separated.
I'm so close
Yet so far
From where I could be
Where I should be.
I cannot enjoy the moments
For fear of wasting them.
Regret stalks me
Like an extension of my own shadow.
I am guilty
For the way the days skim past me
A blur when they should be mine to capture.
But the rope always
Rubs my palms raw.
I'm still letting you win.
And I don't know
How to stop them
Or me.
But the blood continues to drip
Iron and salt mix.

Memories a fabrication.

What is life if not the counting down of hours
As they creep past
Watching the clock hands spin round and round
Filled with dread
Wanting desperately to be somewhere in the brighter future
That was promised
But somehow still pulled towards the rosy tinge of the past?
Why are we incapable of seeing that our memories
Are only a fabrication
Of what we want our lives to have been?

We watch ghosts.

Here the sun shines on my face.
I do not feel the need for space.
Years worn into this path
Skin marred by time
Hand still fits in mine.
Grab tight to certainty
You in this place
Me too
As we watch ghosts
Of memories long past
Marvel at the speed of moments
Racing along like clouds on the wind.

The valley spoke.

Terrain laid bare before me.
No life in sight
Save you and I.
My how loud the quiet sounds
When the relentless thoughts
Finally come up short.
The valley spoke love to me
Void and full of mystery.
All that I could see
And all that I could not
Stretched out together
To meet the horizon.

Bury this hurt here.

Maybe I will always have a little brokenness in me
And maybe you will never quite understand the pain
Of the slow shattering of your past
Like a chandelier falling
That you can never catch.
But I think I will always bury this hurt here with you
Entrust you to guard it,
Nurture my sore soul with your laughter.
Show me that there is more to me than broken glass.

Sinking sun signals.

The sinking sun signals to me
An end or perhaps a beginning
Perspective bent, at the mercy of the horizon.
How shall I consider the rays
That glide effortlessly over this terrain?
Greet me with the golden hour
Glimmering with a beauty untold
A secret the earth has possessed for all time.

Evidence of end.

Surrounded by the giants as they shed this life
For a more dormant season
Reflection crowds me
Rains down in brilliant orange and red.
All around the evidence of end.
But the wind brings promise of more
Dares me to settle in
Warm my hands by the fire
Pull my scarf tight
Wait patiently in the falling night.

Casually bottle.

Maybe I will suffice to fill an idle page
Each day unlock the monotony of the stagnate hour
Give the mind and heart a canvas to spill onto.
Try to make art of the mess others casually bottle.

If I must lose my way.

Someone once asked me what it is
That draws me to stillness?
What appeals to me to embrace silence
Despite the busy noise of the ordinary?
How can I share the way the wind whispers to me?
The chattering of the leaves as they fall
The chilly peace that surrounds
Those that venture to the farthest corners
If I must lose my way to find this
This unspeakable knowledge of space
The idea that there is something far greater
Lying in wait for those that dare to feel
With all that they are
Even if it strips them bare
Leaves them burned by sensation
I will gladly wander into oblivion.
I can only hope that you will accompany me.

Labyrinth.

A labyrinth exists beyond these surface level preoccupations.
Below is a treacherous place
At the mercy of the waves of emotion
That rack my mind incessantly.
I aim to make use of such capacity
That I might dare to delve deeper
Allow myself the prospect
Of uncovering this labyrinth of connection
That exists and appears only to those that care to look
Past the dark hedges that separate one path from another.

Feel it with me.

I am not telling you
Offering glimpses
Of the raging sea within
That you might try
To change me.
I do not need to purge
This feeling lets me see
Clearly the life before me.
I only speak its name
Aloud that you might
Feel it with me.

Unafraid to rebuild.

White blanket above, cloaked us all safe
Hidden in the night below.
Wild sounds from the wood
Became a comfort in spite.
Nothing could mar her more.
The damage was done and
She found herself unafraid to rebuild.
A second chance was all it was.
And if fate might knock yet again
Tear the boards free once more
Well, a third was perhaps a greater blessing.
Shed the weight of circumstance
Free herself from the bonds of remorse
For a life she was never meant to live.

Forced to be a fortress.

I can't help but feel attached to my shadows
The bits of me born in the dark
That spent all those lonely nights
Hearing the lullaby of silent tears
Feeling the tremor of a breaking heart
The bending of a spirit pushed too far
The heartstrings stretched taught to mend within.
These are all a part of my treasured foundation
Hidden away from sight
Forced to be a fortress under this façade.

Part 2: Firelight

Section 3: Finding the Light

Firelight.

I stood encased in heat
As the flames licked my face Singed
my skin to match
The rawness within.

I felt cold wrap around me
Try to pull me back in
Remind me of the chill that
Never quite releases me.

You are the firelight
That made art of the imprint
Of these shadow songs
And silhouettes tinged in crimson.

Each frame casts a different shadow
Sculpted by the elements
Forged from the fading of the light
Brought to life by the dark.

Memories like tremors.

Today I walked down the same path my feet travelled
Hundreds of times.
Most would call this experience coming home,
I call it being a stranger in a familiar land turned foreign.
The bones are the same, the flesh transformed.
I cannot recognize my innocence in this place.
Who was she
The girl who wandered through these woods
Ran free through these hay fields?
How can I ever reclaim her?
I think perhaps she is lost to me.
Just as lost as those endless years
Spanning between the reckoning and now.
I feel the memories like tremors
As they run through my hands.
My feet know their way around
But this is not the home I grew in.
This is a bittersweet reminder that time is relentless.
The world simply continues to turn.
The tides change even if I do not stand watch as they do.
I wish I could still see you.
My childhood bedroom forever a locked door.
I will never feel her again.
She's buried too deep.
The tears sting in my eyes, but they don't fall this time.
Is this healing?
Somehow it hurts more than I thought it would.
Have I finally come to terms with the tragedy of this place?
Can I finally be free to mourn her
The girl I was, the girl I could have been, the girl I left behind?
But maybe I walked away for her
To save the only piece of us that I could.

Like sand upon the wind.

Time is like sand upon the wind.
I can't seem to get a handle on it.
I do not feel the single moments
Rather it is everything all at once
Comingled to overwhelm my senses
Spread across endless days
A cloudy reminder
At the end of my vision
That I am missing far more
For the sake of trying to hold it all.

A refuge and a cage.

Crushed under the burden of these thoughts
I swear I can hear the snap of cracking ribs.
You tell me it is only the beating of my heart
Echoing deep in my own depths,
Assure me that my lungs were made for this.
Breath is not stolen from me
Nor is it something I must guard.
You see, it sneaks up on me
Hides in the corner waiting for conversation to falter.
The quiet is both a refuge and a cage.
Somehow you are always there
Helping me support the weight
Giving me space to breathe once more.

Enough.

Enough.
All you wanted.
All you feared you could never be.
All you were all along.

Forgive you at a distance.

I will not let myself fall to your level
Will not crouch among the undergrowth
Just to see you slither in deceit.

I will do you a kindness
Forgive you at a distance
Lest the gardener purge this place.

I'll pace on the terrace
Keep watch as you scrabble
Pick up the pieces for the sake of those left behind.

Tore you free.

A soul of swirled color
A hue unexplained
You were everything
And nothing all the same.

I could not grasp you
Lacked the feel of you
Fingertips coming up short
But you were everywhere.

You were overwhelming
Suffocating and encompassing
A darkness I could not expel
Unescapable, my own shadow.

Until one day I tripped in the sunlight
Tore you free from my sole
Felt the light spread over me.
The air tasted sweeter without you.

To simplify things.

To simplify things
You can call me a dreamer.
I won't burden you
With the contradictory windings
Of my mind.

I am poised
To unravel in an instant
But perhaps that is precisely
What makes this moment so
Preciously extraordinary.

We are all destined to fall apart.
Why should we not marvel
At the time we spend
So perfectly, fragilely held together?
After all, time gives meaning to all things.

There are brief moments
When you are effortlessly yourself
Despite what the world tells you.
Cherish those moments.
Chase them
For all you're worth.

I have not learned her language yet.

Hopes and dreams used to flow like lava
Rush onto paper in the form of poetry
Smoking pen as the heat coursed from my fingers
The only alternative to succumbing to the flame.

Now my inspiration comes slow
Like concrete poured after it has already
Began to set. I worry, as I always have
That maybe there is nothing left to be said.

But the wind still caresses my face.
The coming storm still teases my bones
With an electric reminder that we are
Meant to be conductors of magic.

So I wait, as only I can. For the magic
To return that I might put into words
This mystery that curls through my veins.
She has always been there
I just haven't learned her language yet.

The raindrops that mar my page
Are evidence of the heavens
Promising life and purpose to the thoughts
I cannot yet taste.

Bend the light.

Society aims to bend the light, manipulate your sight.
Whispers say your differences are weaknesses
You must bury them, deep.
No one mentioned that digging that grave would bring
Much darker insecurities to the surface.

I keep tripping over misconceptions as I spend my days
Looking back at the path I traveled yesterday
Searching for dangers from my past.
How much of my present have I forfeited
Caught up in fear, scanning memory for regret?

Today I want to be unapologetic
Embrace the unique even if it is considered weak.
I'll fortify them, build a stronghold
Form a foundation from the words that used to tear me down.
Tell myself I am more. Maybe actually believe it.

Soaking in the immensity.

Fingertips gripped tight to the grass carpet
Soaking in the immensity of it all
Surrounded by endless sky and
Cascading hills as far as the horizon
And farther still.

That's the thing about horizons and sight
The knowledge that it continues beyond
But never quite grasping the meaning.

Everything has its horizon
You. Me. The sea.
It's the dropping over the edge that
Leaves us all sweetly terrified of more.

Blurred edges and open minds
Trust your senses and your connection
To this concept of more.

Chase the thrill
The same kind that used to have you
Sprinting wide open through a field under
The full moon's watchful eye
Blind in the night but clear of mind.

To search for a solution.

Some days I am a flame
Untamed, burning so bright
That others must take a step back
Think twice before they draw close.

Other days I am a cold winter night
Beautifully void and brutal
Others would not dare join me
Standing on the edge defying this harsh wind.

You see I realize now I never needed to search for a solution
The answer was within me all along.
I am my own thaw, my own cooling.
Nature must run its course, even my own.

I used to think that the search was the meaning
Constantly looking for a way to smooth out the difference.
Maybe unstable is just the dark shadow cast on liveliness.
Now, I just need to live. For myself. For once.

Aligning.

There are small moments dotted through a lifetime
When the world feels just right
The perplexing notion that you are perhaps
Right where you were meant to be
Running the race right on course
Keeping pace brilliantly
With your own heart's ticking
Like the aligning of a clock and an hourglass.

For me that is a particularly pleasant day trip
To a sleepy mountain town
With an inexplicably charming café
Or a lazy morning in a cabin
Warmed by wood fire
Perfectly out of touch with the world,
Absorbed in your own.

This is passion.

Maybe you'll go mad without it.
Or maybe you'll make sense of
The madness living under your own skin.
Or maybe it will drive you mad
Then push you farther still.
People fear what they cannot control
But this is passion.
So run with the madness darling.
Create in the moments between sanity.

Uncharted.

This road I walk is uncharted
The gravel beneath my feet brand new.
I do not have tracks to follow
Not here, not anymore.
But the terrain is promising
Of a land lush with opportunity
That I might find some meaning beyond.
So my soles may ache a few months more
Years perhaps I will trek in the wilderness
But somewhere, someday
I will find shelter.
More than that, I believe
I will find solace and splendor
Far beyond the fruitless march
I will find freedom and even joy
In the sun rays as they force their way through the trees
A sky wide-open and a beauty so rare
I might never dream again
A life that is cherished and a purpose fulfilled.
But for now I will wander
Lost but not aimless
Searching and seeking the shelter waiting for me.

Picture you glorious.

It is time.
Shake the weariness from your fragile frame.
Yes, now is the time.
Pick yourself up off that cold granite tile of the bathroom floor.
No matter what you think the leak
That created this saltwater lake cannot consume you.

You are your own lifeboat.
Trust me, you'll float.
High above the cascades, you'll find the strength
To grip the corners of that vanity and switch off the faucet.

You are fighting for more than yourself.
It is for the countless strangers
That watch from the shadows
Decide to cling to your life for inspiration
Picture you glorious rising from the ashes
Rather than broken among the rubble.

Crash against the light.

Expectations like shadows on the ground
Swell and stretch with the fading light
Until the clock chimes midnight.
Your shadow is swallowed up by the oblivion of the night.

What if the absence of the shadow
That your presence cast is more
Than just the sun sliding beneath the horizon?

What if shadows crash against the light
Like the ocean against the shore at high tide?

Let is rise.

I can feel it
Seething inside
Beyond description
Normally attributed to
The swelling of emotion.
See I have not given into it.
I have let it rise
Push me up to mountain tops
Belief in the power
The right
To feel free of constraints
Especially those others
Try to force on me.

Reckless.

Cigarette smoke and scenery
The kind of reckless
I knew I could never be.
Still, you saw me.
All of me
Even the parts
The world stripped from me.
I saw you too
The vulnerable brokenness
Of me reflected in you.
Whole for a moment
As we spoke of its existence
For once, briefly acknowledging it
Rather than trying to snuff it out
Hide it within the parts
More easily accepted.
The kind of free
That is reckless to be,
You showed that to me.

Read the secrets.

This world is relentless
Always trying to steal your magic
But I still remember the heat
Radiating off the pavement.
It left a slight sting on my skin
As it sank into my bones
Made me feel like I too had a fire inside
Like the stars burning in the night sky.

How many times can we truly say
We feel infinite?
Isn't that chase of such moments
The whole point
To feel grand but insignificant
To appreciate the abyss of immensity?
Dig down deep, read the secrets
Inscribed on your own roots.

Embrace the bitter.

Do not shy away from your strangeness
The kind you catch glimpses of in the mirror.
Embrace the bitter undertone.
You are free to be more than the sweetness
They have labeled you.
Someday you will see it
That same strangeness reflected
So purposefully in another.
The gift of a new chance
To appreciate not just what it is that sets you apart
But also what has brought you together.

The stars saw both paths.

I suppose the stars saw both paths as worthy
Charted in a way as to collide, to grow, to soothe,
To learn from one another.

There are those that see things in fire.
Sometimes, I envy their ability
To scorch the souls of strangers with words
That burn into the page
Flames that climb up their thoughts
Warmth to cut the chill of the night.

I am one of the others, those that see things in water.
The churning darkness of oblivion
Beckons me to be swallowed by it
To feel the fullness of the ocean within me
Waves as they crash against my ribs
Seek out the moonlit path to guide me home.

It's only golden.

Golden
Was the day
I finally trusted you to stay.

Golden
Like the rays
On that crisp winter day.

Golden
Was the sand
Of that secret beach at the end of an overgrown road forgotten.

Golden
Is the hue
Of my soul and every day.
Since you
I have forgotten what it is to feel gray.

It's only golden.

Polish then pass by.

This life is full of poor circumstance
And disappointment of shocking degree.
May the pain polish then pass by
Like the flowing of a river that carves a canyon
Shape you new and mighty
Evidence that you survived
Were not worn away to nothing
Born anew with a majesty inside.

The sun will rise all the same.

Some days the pain comes in waves.
I lay on the shore wide awake
Ready to grasp precious air in the break.
But I've learned in this life
That no matter how rough the seas get
The sun will rise all the same
Beat down on me with refreshing intensity.

When the days are endless
And the moon rise merely brings
More intimacy to your own torture
Remember that time, if it be so merciful
Will bring healing to the most battered of bones.

Section 4: The Mending

Distance.

Just beyond my grasp
Precisely where it has always been
The sweet illusion of contentment
Illusive rest for this weary soul.

Time has forged a tight seal
And a knowledge that strength is born from pain.
It took years to learn to appreciate my own brokenness
To realize the cracks and scars that mark me
Are evidence of a struggle that is distinctly mine.

I am proud of the distance
Between now and yesterday.

The blaze you crave.

If you want it
There are times you must chase it.
We cannot expect it to find us
In our own circumstance.
So grab it rough
Breathe life to it like a flame.
Do not be afraid
To strike the match yourself.
Set the blaze you crave.

Undeniably aware.

Those moments when the universe
Makes you undeniably aware
Of your own mortality
The flash of memory long buried
A beating in your chest so strong
You'd think your bones not fit to contain it

What if we lived like that
With all that we are up on a ledge?
No time for excuses.
No promise of a moment more.
Could we then realize
True freedom lies
In the embrace of what we have held
Inside ourselves all this time?

Wells.

If we are all wells
I pray you are not afraid to drown in me
As I have in you,
That I might smile as your waters slip over my head
Feel the peace and breathlessness of another's depths.
As you rush into me, I to you.

They do not define.

You should know
I am here
Hidden beneath all my fears and
The bitterness that has held me captive.
I never tried to hide these scars.
They are mine.
I will own them every time
But they do not define.
I am more,
More than the devastation
That led me to my madness.

Alloy.

When my edges begin to blur
Melt into yours like the pouring of two metals
I hope that we are stronger bonded together
Impervious to the corrosion that many succumb to,
That we might marvel at the alloy we have forged
Rather than search to see our boundaries as before.

Bursting at the seams.

I am stitched together
With thread made of hopes and dreams.
We often forget the strain
This life puts on such fragile string.

This world fills our minds
With anxieties and woes we never knew we had.
They say we must have buried them deep,
But you know better.

We never worried until they told us we should,
Never felt shame until they said we should be sorry.
Now, here we are
Bursting at the seams.

Trying desperately to hold ourselves together,
Keep from unraveling, don't spill the ocean for them to see.
Fear not, brave one, freedom comes
With the pulling of a thread.

Sharing the light.

I have always felt a bit out of place in this frame,
Skin and bones a structure that seemed a bit off.
This journey to find myself is tiresome
But the destination is worthy
To not shy away from strangers
Not endlessly search for an empty supermarket aisle
Walk with purpose down a city street
Actually believe I have a right to occupy it.

I used to apologize
For everything, constantly.
What am I so sorry for anyway?
Nothing. Not anymore.
These years are short
Too short to try to please them all,
Too short to harbor such resentment and pain.
Now this path is one of finding happiness
And sharing that light with other lost souls.

Lose your way.

Do not fit willingly to the mold
Palms pressed to the walls.
Will them to break.
Chase only what is true
To you and your heart.
Don't be consumed
By the irrational need
To seem like you belong.
Maybe you don't.
But you are strong,
Strong enough
To make your own place.
There is no perfect time
To step from the path
Lose your way in the wilderness
For the glorious pursuit of yourself.
There is only now.

Bright.

I know that we too will fade with time,
But I promise to burn bright with you
While we can.

The other side.

When the light grows faint
And you cannot quite feel
The heat of the sun
That once kissed your skin.
When you crave to be scorched
If just to feel alive again.

Remember the brightness within,
The shine that has guided you
Through endless nights before.
Think of your love of the moonlight
The pale glow of the unknown
That gave you the strength
To push on through tangled
Thickets miles deep
To find yourself free
On the other side.

There is always another side.

A foothold for you too.

Hope is not a flat surface.
There are nooks and crannies
Curves and corners
To grasp.
We all fall at some point
But you will eventually hit hope.
Don't fear the slide.
There is a foothold for you too.
You just have to feel for it.

Worthy.

I was forced to grow
Long before I felt ready,
Not that we ever really do.
I found myself
Squeezing through the cracks
Of black pavement
Clouding my view
Choking off sunlight.
I knew
Freedom felt necessary
Drove me on to face the winds.
The surface was cruel
But beautiful.
Worthy was the struggle.
So was I.

Intend to be heard.

Brave one, speak loud.
Speak truth.
Speak like you intend to be heard.

Someday you will realize
There is a beauty in you
That circumstance and calamity
Can never steal away.
You hold a wild heart
At the core of you.
You may not be tamed by force
Only you can be freely given
To the worthy few.
You were destined to run free
Escape your bonds
Before you were even aware of them
Rubbing ankles and wrists raw
From the unconscious
Effort and striving
For so much more than
These four walls and final says
From those that did not
Have the right or the means
To try to muzzle you.

Etched into my bones.

At the end of this life
Will I find the details of you
Etched into my bones?
Will mine be there on yours?
A rude mark to the fading of time,
Evidence of a love
That a lifetime could not contain.

Too deep a hold on me.

I used to think the secret
To moving past this would be
Finding a way to shut it out,
That the problem was the growth of such feeling
Allowing the hurt too deep a hold on me
Roots anchored to the cellar walls.
If I could only find a way
To keep it hidden in the shadows
That it might wither without the light of day.
But it did not wither
It sat stubbornly
Found sustenance in other ways
Starved the flowers I labored over
Left me void of all color
Alone to feed it in the dark.

There I realized
We all have a right to feel
Every bit of what we are given
For as long as it may take
And as deep as it may ache
To be shaped by it,
To grow from it.

Healing comes through acknowledgment.
Avoidance only lets it fester inside
Leaves you unknowingly at its mercy.
So I will not apologize or feel shame
For a depth that still exists in me
I will allow it to grow,
Let my tears nourish this ground.

The love we do have.

Maybe somewhere along the way
We will learn that dwelling on the love
We do not have
Will never fill the absence we feel.
The only way past it,
The only way to wholeness
Is to recognize the love we do have,
The love we take for granted
The love we overlook
The love that has been here all along
Even if that love must come from within.

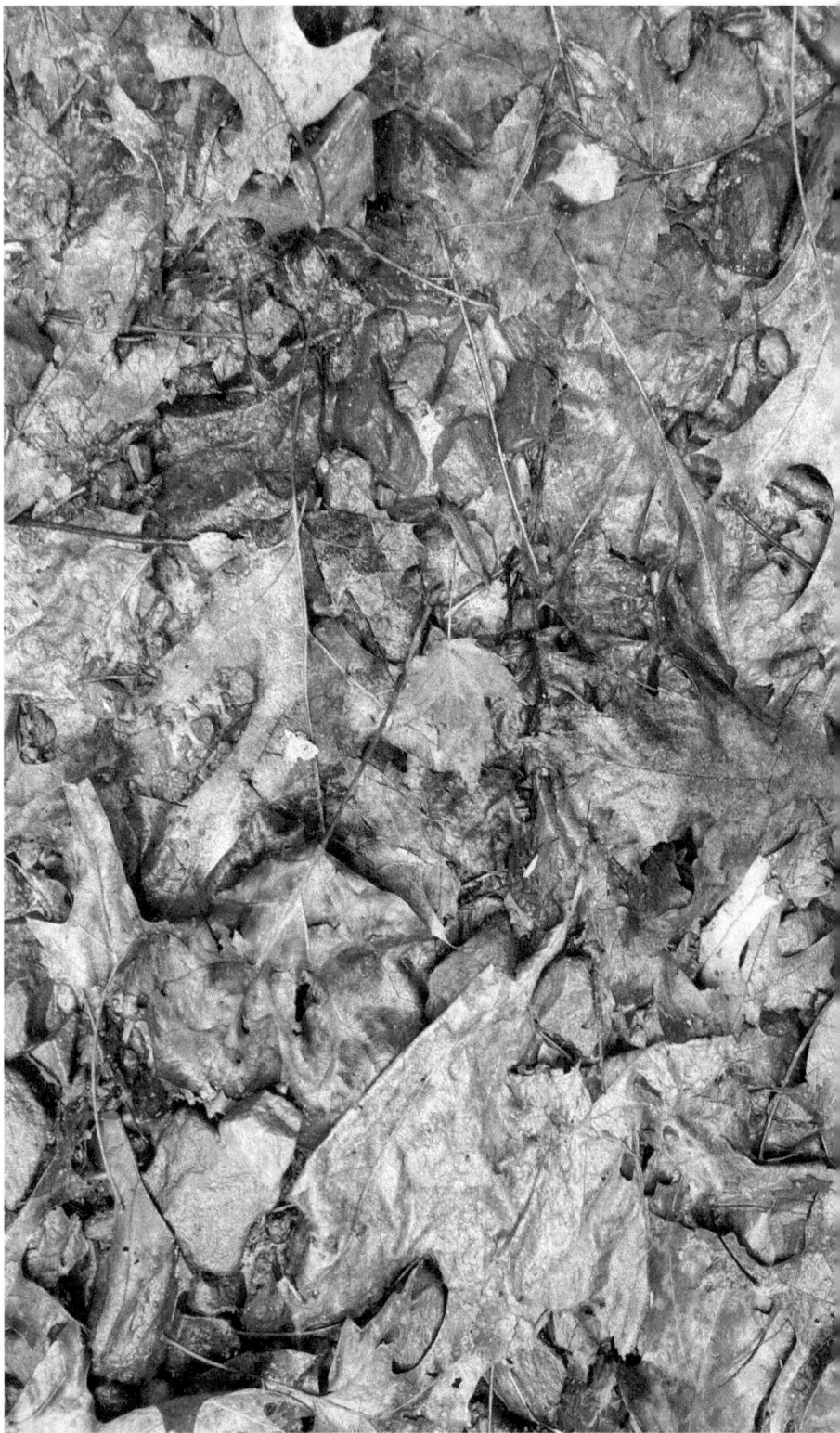

Clear water.

Clear water
You are crystal to me.
The sweet flood
That clears my vision
Stings my eyes so that
I might see past
The dust that is my own making.
You quench my drought
The one that I have brought upon myself.
You bring out the good,
Give life to those who
Only knew death.
Hope is liquid,
Crystal clear.
It flows
All around those
Whose vision has been cleared.

More.

Years. I have lived years
And never truly tasted
The sweet nectar of life
Until you.
You make me want more,
To see it. To feel it. To be it.
More in every way
Uncontained, dizzying possibility and
Thrill of what may come.
So, with you I will
Walk miles above the rushing water
With no fear of falling.
I'll trust this narrow platform to hold
Walk this same path
That history has told.
I won't fear the rattle
Of traffic overhead.
I'll laugh with the wind
As she pushes at my back.

Sturdy enough to build.

I remember you before I knew you to be mine,
Before it was obvious that our lives should be entwined.
I did not know then how to appreciate the intricate working
The slow forging of a friendship
Sturdy enough to build so much more.
I thank the heavens
You were the architect we needed,
For I could not have crafted this love alone.

Heart of my heart.

I know that I will never
Let the heart of my heart
Feel that they are less.
No force shall make them
Feel separate from me.
As long as breath is within me
I will know them.
And they too will know
That they are known
By a heart that breaks
Each dawn to sew itself back together
Each evening for the shear
Pleasure to be broken
Yet again.

Every soul is woven.

One day my whispers will sound off these mountain tops
And I will no longer be told
To raise my voice.

All will hear the echo of the ink
As it drips from my fingers
Paints the picture my bones beg for me to pour forth.

See I am bound by something deeper
The idea that every soul is woven
With a unique pattern to be shared.

I do not yet know the compounds of my contribution,
But the quilt shall hold the evidence
Of a life intended to be lived well.

Not meant to be generic.

Hope is not meant to be generic
A subscription passed meaninglessly
From the lips of strangers.
The genuine hope lies in the clearing
Remains after the haze has lifted.
It is the beacon to which
Your feet cannot help but follow
Through marshlands and deserts alike.
It is hard won
The unearthing of oneself,
But far sweeter than
The assumption that the same hope
Is carried within us all.
For when the fog lifts
Your true hope will be revealed.

More dreams than you had to spare.

Someday the earth will be left upturned
Where the life you envisioned
The one you wished so desperately into existence
Fell tired and true to meet reality.
This life will not be what you thought it would.
How could it, when you cannot see beyond the now?
The outcome is not one you will see coming
But it shall be worthy
Of more dreams than you had to spare.

Window pane.

I listened as the earth breathed to me in echoes
Felt the rush of the wind beneath these stripped wings.
The rustle of the leaves told me secrets from beyond.
I heard the truth lost in translation
Embraced by a beauty I could not see.
It spoke to me
Of hours past, moments collected like broken glass
Formed a window pane of precious memories
Shattered by the stones carelessly cast.
But the shards are with us still
Floating like confetti on the wind
Dust of humanity and the grace that cannot be lost.
No, time will not destroy you,
Only alter your state.
Your foundation, the compounds of you
Are ever sacred, never wasted.
You were meant to be you
In all your forms
For all your days.

Thank you for braving the shadows to seek the light with me.

The journey continues.

@erica_adelaidepoetry